MORE 10-MINUTE DEVOTIONS FOR YOUTH GROUPS

Group Books

Loveland, Colorado

More 10-Minute Devotions for Youth Groups
Copyright © 1992 by Group Publishing, Inc.

Credits
Edited by Lois Keffer
Designed by Judy Bienick
Contributors: Dean Feldmeyer, Mike Gillespie, Margaret Hinchey, Mike and Amy Nappa, Jolene Roehlkepartain, Yvonne Steindal, Steve and Annie Wamberg, Paul Woods, Christine Yount

Library of Congress Cataloging-in-Publication Data
More 10-minute devotions for youth groups / [edited by Lois Keffer; contributors Dean Feldmeyer... et al.].
     p.   cm.
     ISBN 1-55945-068-1
     1. Youth—Prayer-books and devotions—English.
I. Keffer, Lois.   II. Feldmeyer, Dean, 1951- .   III. Title:
More ten-minute devotions for youth groups.
BV4850.M665 1992
242'.63—dc20
                                        91-42395
                                           CIP

13 12 11 10 9 8   05 04 03 02 01 00 99

Printed in the United States of America.

Visit our Web site: www.grouppublishing.com

Contents

Introduction 7

10-MINUTE Devotions on Personal Spiritual Growth

Anxieties Aweigh! 12
Anxiety, fear

Who Cares? 13
Apathy

Follow the Leader 14
Discipleship, following Jesus

Goal to Go 15
Goal-setting

Keys to Your Future 17
Grades, learning

Honest or Bogus? 18
Honesty, integrity

Joyfully Yours 20
Joy

Gimme, Gimme, Gimme 21
Materialism, greed

Stick It Out! 22
Patience, perseverance

Who's the Boss? 23
Self-control

What Do You See? 25
Self-image

Stressed Out! 26
Stress

Poison—Beware! 27
Substance abuse

The Fear of Failure 28
Success, failure

Making Change 30
Transitions

1 0-MINUTE Devotions on Christ-Centered Relationships

Oh Brother, Oh Sister!. 34
Brothers and sisters

The Art of Compromise 37
Conflicts

Family Tension 39
Family, parents

Oops! 40
Forgiveness

The Friendship Factor. 42
Friendship

Come Join Us! 43
Including others

Your Eyes Can Fool You 44
Judging

Everyone Wins! 47
Loving enemies

You Heard What?. 48
Peace-making

Choosing Teams 51
Peer influence

5-Minute Servants 52
Servanthood

Timing Is Everything. 53
Sexuality

Too Good to Keep 55
Witnessing, sharing faith

1 0-MINUTE Devotions on Faith Issues

Get an Attitude. 58
Church

Believe It or Not! 59
Doubts

Stompin' Stewards 61
Earth, creation

It Hurts to Say Goodbye 63
Grief

Aiming for Hope 65
Hope
Finding the Balance 67
Justice, mercy
Risky Business 69
Love
Haves and Have Nots 70
Missions
Slow Down 71
Rest
I'm Clean! 72
Sin, forgiveness
Use It or Lose It 73
Stewardship
Hide 'n' Seek 74
Time With God
Look Ahead 75
Vocation, future

1 0-MINUTE Devotions for Special Occasions

New Year, New You 78
New Year's Day
Living Valentines 80
Valentine's Day
Washed Clean 81
Lent
Egg-ceptional Surprise! 82
Easter
Bringing Joy to Parents 83
Mother's Day, Father's Day
To Win the Prize 85
Graduation
R & R 87
Summer vacation
Be Prepared 88
New school year
A Note of Thanks 90
Thanksgiving
Get Ready! 92
Advent
What's in a Name? 94
Christmas

Introduction

The enthusiastic response to *10-Minute Devotions for Youth Groups* highlighted the need for quick devotions that help kids understand and apply God's Word. So here's a fresh batch of fast and easy ideas you'll use to spice up Bible studies, wrap up meetings or add deeper meaning to any activity with kids. Each devotion is designed to be ready in minutes—whenever you want to grab your kids' attention for a special lesson... or cap your time together with an experience your teenagers will remember.

DEVOTION ELEMENTS

Each devotion consists of the following seven elements.

■ **Theme:** This is the topic of the devotion, the main thought. Themes cover a variety of teenagers' needs and concerns.

■ **Scripture:** Each devotion is based on scripture that supports the theme and shows kids that God is concerned about every area of their lives.

■ **Overview:** This brief statement describes the devotion and tells what the participants will learn.

■ **Preparation:** This part describes exactly what materials you'll need for the devotion and what you'll need to do to prepare for it.

When preparing for the devotions, remember to involve the young people themselves. They can help round up supplies, but they can also help lead. The devotions are easy to follow and easy to prepare. Even busy teenagers can find time to prepare and lead these quick devotions. Involving teenagers as much as possible gives them ownership of the devotion and helps them develop leadership skills they will keep their whole lives.

■ **Experience:** Each devotion contains a unique element that lets kids actually experience the theme. Kids use their senses of sight, hearing, smell, touch and taste to gain a deeper understanding of the topic being discussed.

All activities can be adapted to fit the size of your group. If you have a small group, simply do the devotional activities together. If you have a larger group, divide into small groups using a variety of methods. For example, you can divide into small groups by eye color, hair color or birthdays. Or you can spell the theme for the devotion. If the theme is love, have the group members sound off by spelling "love." All "l's" form one group, all "o's" form another group, and so on.

■ *Response:* Participants take the experience one step further by thinking about what they've experienced and how it applies to their lives. They think about and discuss their discoveries.

■ *Closing:* Each devotion concludes with a prayer or activity that summarizes the devotional thought and helps kids apply it to their lives.

THE FOUR SECTIONS

The devotions in this book are divided into four sections for easy reference.

● **10-Minute Devotions on Personal Spiritual Growth**—Some of the themes in this section are self-control, discipleship, honesty, stress, joy and self-image.

● **10-Minute Devotions on Christ-Centered Relationships**—Themes in this section range from friendships and family relationships to relationships with the world. Your kids will discuss judging, including others, servanthood, brothers and sisters, peace-making and sexuality.

● **10-Minute Devotions on Faith Issues**—Your group will explore themes such as love, sin, doubts, stewardship, justice and God's creation.

● **10-Minute Devotions for Special Occasions**—These themes will put new meaning into special times like Christmas, Mother's Day, Father's Day, summer vacation, Lent and Easter.

Be sure to look through the themes in this section. Some of the devotions can be used throughout the year as well as on special occasions. For example, "Get Ready!" on page 92 can be used for Advent or any time during the year you want to stress the idea of preparing for God to work in kids' lives.

Feel free to be creative with *More 10-Minute Devotions for Youth Groups*. Go ahead and adapt any of the quick devotions to fit a particular situation or need. And reach for this book any time, anywhere—to share fun, meaningful times that lead your kids into deeper walks with God.

10-Minute Devotions on Personal Spiritual Growth

Anxieties Aweigh!

■ **Theme:** Anxiety, fear
■ **Scripture:** 1 Peter 5:6-7
■ **Overview:** Group members will experience anxiety and help each other discover ways to give anxieties to God.
■ **Preparation:** Set up a circle of chairs. Have a CD- or cassette player ready to play one of your group's favorite Christian songs. Bring enough colored paper for each person to have one sheet. You will also need a Bible and a wastebasket.

EXPERIENCE

When kids have gathered, play a quick game of musical chairs. If you have more than 12 kids, have two fewer chairs than participants for each round. Let the music run for only five to 10 seconds before you stop it. Play three or four quick rounds. Then ask: How did you feel when you were waiting for the music to stop? How are those feelings like the anxieties you feel in life? What do you do about fears and anxieties?

RESPONSE

Have someone read 1 Peter 5:6-7 aloud. Then give each person a piece of colored paper. Have kids each tear their paper into something representing one source of anxiety in their life. Ask volunteers to show and explain their torn-paper symbols. Have the rest of the group suggest ways they might cast those anxieties on the Lord. If your group members all know each other well, encourage everyone to share.

CLOSING

Form pairs. Read 1 Peter 5:6-7 again, and have partners each give their torn-paper anxiety symbol to their partner. Then have kids each crush their partner's anxiety symbol into a ball and throw it in a wastebasket, representing how God can wipe out our anxieties. Close your session with prayer encouraging kids to give their fears and anxieties to God. ■

Who Cares?

■ **Theme:** Apathy
■ **Scripture:** Revelation 3:15-16
■ **Overview:** Group members will experience trying to accomplish something in an apathetic setting, and suggest ways to avoid being apathetic.
■ **Preparation:** Make arrangements for kids to meet at an appropriate place after the meeting, such as a restaurant or someone's house. You'll need a Bible.

EXPERIENCE

Take two volunteers aside and tell them it's their job to convince the rest of the group that everyone should get together at a place you suggest following the meeting. Send the volunteers out of the room for 30 seconds to develop their strategy. While the volunteers are away, tell the other kids to act apathetic about the volunteers' suggestions by yawning, looking around the room or staring at the ceiling. Bring the volunteers back and let them try to get the others excited about going out after the meeting.

RESPONSE

Ask someone to read Revelation 3:15-16 aloud. Discuss what this passage tells us about God's attitude toward apathy.

Ask the volunteers how it felt to be in the middle of such apathy. Ask the others how they felt during the exercise. Say: Apathy hurts progress. It also hurts relationships.

CLOSING

Have students take turns suggesting one thing they can do to show people around them that they aren't apathetic. Then announce that you really are gathering at "the appointed place" after the meeting! Say: Remember that Jesus isn't apathetic about anybody. See if you can help someone understand that this week by your attitude toward him or her. ■

Follow the Leader

■ **Theme:** Discipleship, following Jesus
■ **Scripture:** Matthew 16:24
■ **Overview:** Kids will participate in a crazy walk and compare that experience to following Jesus.
■ **Preparation:** You'll need a Bible.

EXPERIENCE

Form two groups. Have each group appoint a leader who will make up a crazy style of walking. For example, leaders can swing one foot out, flap their arms, lean to one side, make a noise with each step, or do any combination of the above.

Have the leaders line up their groups; teach them the "crazy walk"; then say, "Walk this way!" and lead the groups outside. Have leaders take their groups around the church then crazy-walk their way back to the youth room. Have kids sit down and discuss how it felt to crazy-walk in front of other people.

RESPONSE

Have a volunteer read Matthew 16:24 aloud. Ask: How is following Jesus like crazy-walking? How is it different? How are your feelings about crazy-walking in front of others like the way you feel when you choose to follow Jesus instead of following your non-Christian friends? Ask kids to tell about specific times they felt as if they stood out from the crowd because of their Christian choices and behavior.

CLOSING

Say: Being a follower of Jesus isn't always easy. But it's always the right thing to do. And it has its rewards!

Ask kids to share some of the rewards that come from following Christ—both now and in the future. Then close with prayer, thanking Jesus for the opportunity to be his followers and asking for strength to follow him in all situations.

Encourage kids to crazy-walk as they leave. ■

Goal to Go

■ **Theme:** Goal-setting
■ **Scripture:** Philippians 3:7-14
■ **Overview:** Group members will learn the purpose of goals and how persistence can help in reaching their personal goals.
■ **Preparation:** For every two people gather 12 cotton balls, two bowls, a spoon and a blindfold. You'll also need a watch with a second hand and a Bible.

EXPERIENCE

Briefly discuss what a goal is. Talk about games that use the term "goal" to describe a score, such as hockey or soccer. Explain that you're going to give everyone a goal to strive for in the next few minutes.

Form pairs. Have one member of each pair put on a blindfold. Tell the non-blindfolded partner to remain totally silent until you give the signal that it's okay to talk. Place a spoon, an empty bowl and a bowl containing 12 cotton balls in front of each blindfolded partner. Explain that the goal is for the blindfolded partner to move the cotton balls from one bowl to the next within a minute and a half, using only the spoon. The other partner can only watch (in agony and frustration) for the first minute. After one minute, tell the sighted partners they can begin coaching with words, but cannot touch the spoons, bowls, cotton balls or their partners. Call time after another 30 seconds. Then let kids remove their blindfolds. Have partners count their cotton balls and report how close they came to their goal.

RESPONSE

Ask both the blindfolded and sighted partners how it felt to try to reach their goal. Ask: How were your frustrations like the frustrations that face us when we try to reach goals in real life?

Have a group member read aloud Philippians 3:7-14. Ask: How can we set goals that are pleasing to God? What does

Goal to Go

Paul's example teach us about what it takes to reach our goals? How can we deal with the frustrations that come along when we're trying to reach our goals? What helps us keep going?

CLOSING

Close by leading the group in this prayer: Lord, I do not know what lies ahead of me. But I do know that your hand is guiding me and your love is supporting me. Help me to set goals that are pleasing to you and then to hang in there until I reach them. Amen. ■

Keys to Your Future

- **Theme:** Grades, learning
- **Scripture:** Proverbs 8:10; 15:14
- **Overview:** Group members will relate keys to knowledge and choose one new thing to learn about in the coming year.
- **Preparation:** You will need Bibles, a small container, pencils and paper.

EXPERIENCE

As kids arrive, ask them to give you whatever keys they're carrying. Place the keys in a container. (If some people don't have keys, that's okay.) Display the key rings one by one. Ask kids to guess what each key is for and who owns it.

Read the two verses from Proverbs in unison. Ask kids why they think God wants them to learn and gain new knowledge. Ask how learning and gaining knowledge is similar to having a set of keys in their pockets. Discuss what kinds of doors knowledge opens.

RESPONSE

Distribute pencils and paper. Have kids each draw the outline of a large key and within it draw or write about three things they would like to learn about in the coming year. These can be related to such things as school, family, career and friends.

Have volunteers share their drawings. Discuss how learning something new is like adding a new key to a key ring. Say: Just as a key will let you open a door or start a car, knowledge will unlock a new area of your life. Without learning, life would be dull and disappointing.

CLOSING

Ask students each to tell which thing in their key drawing is most important to them to learn. Close with sentence prayers like this: Dear God, help me as I try to learn more about _____ in the coming year. For example, someone might say, "Dear God, help me as I learn more about being an auto mechanic in the coming year." ■

Honest or Bogus?

■ **Theme:** Honesty, integrity

■ **Scripture:** Proverbs 12:22

■ **Overview:** Group members will evaluate their own honesty and commit to being more honest.

■ **Preparation:** Write "Totally Honest" and "Totally Bogus" on sheets of newsprint. Put the signs on opposite walls of the room. Write "50%" on a sheet of paper and tape it to the floor midway between the two signs. You'll need copies of the "Honest or Bogus?" handout, pencils and a Bible.

EXPERIENCE

Distribute "Honest or Bogus?" handouts and pencils. Instruct kids to complete the handouts as honestly as possible in two minutes. Then call out the numbers of the situations on the handout. Have kids each stand in a position between the two signs that indicates how they responded. While they're still standing in their positions, ask: What makes it hard to be honest in this situation?

RESPONSE

Ask someone to read Proverbs 12:22 aloud. Talk about the importance of having a reputation for being honest. Then ask kids what it takes to establish and keep a reputation for honesty with their parents, friends and teachers.

Have kids each think of one area in which they think they could be more honest. Ask volunteers to share their responses.

CLOSING

Ask kids to pray silently, making a commitment to be honest in the areas they just thought about. Close the session in spoken prayer asking God's help in keeping these commitments. ■

HONEST OR BOGUS?

Be honest as you place yourself on the "Honest/Bogus" scale below. How honest or bogus would you be in these situations?

TOTALLY HONEST_____TOTALLY BOGUS
100% 90% 80% 70% 60% 50% 60% 70% 80% 90% 100%

1. You're home an hour-and-a-half late from a date, but your parents are asleep. The next morning, how honest are you when they ask how well you kept curfew?

2. You're telling your friends about something that happened to you when they weren't around. Do you stretch the details to make the story more interesting? Where do you put yourself on the "Honest/Bogus" scale?

3. In a mild panic, you've made a date with your "second choice" to the big dance at school. How honest are you with your date about where he or she stands with you?

4. To cheat or not to cheat: that is the question, because you spaced out instead of studying for a big test. Are you honest or bogus in the classroom that day?

5. You're allowed a certain amount of food for private consumption at your fast-food job. How likely are you to sneak a bag of burgers for your friends? Rate yourself on the "Honest/Bogus" scale.

Joyfully Yours

▰▰▰▰▰▰▰▰▰▰▰▰

■ **Theme:** Joy
■ **Scripture:** John 15:9-11
■ **Overview:** Group members will explore what brings joy to their lives and discuss what Jesus says about the source of joy.
■ **Preparation:** Gather paper, pencils, scissors and a Bible.

EXPERIENCE

Give kids each a piece of paper. Have pencils and scissors available. Say: In the next three minutes, I want you to create something with this paper that symbolizes what brings joy to you. You can tear the paper, draw on it or cut it.

After three minutes call time and have kids share their paper projects. Then ask: Do you see any similarities in the things that bring joy to all of you?

Say: Now close your eyes and think back on a moment in your life when you experienced a deep sense of joy. Think about where you were and what brought it about.

After a few moments of silence, ask volunteers to share their joyful experiences. Again, discuss similarities.

RESPONSE

Have a volunteer read aloud John 15:9-11. Ask: What does Jesus say will bring joy to our lives? How do the experiences we've shared fit with Jesus' teaching?

CLOSING

Say: Happiness comes and goes depending on our moods, the weather, how others treat us—lots of things. But when we follow Jesus' teaching, joy lives in us and cannot be removed.

Close by singing "I Have the Joy" or "The Joy of the Lord Is My Strength." ■

Gimme, Gimme, Gimme

■ **Theme:** Materialism, greed

■ **Scripture:** Hebrews 13:5

■ **Overview:** Group members will experience what it's like to get a lot of something and then protect it. Kids will then think about things they always want more of.

■ **Preparation:** Gather two stacks of old newspapers, a marker, some newsprint and a Bible.

EXPERIENCE

Form two teams. Give each team a stack of newspaper. Send the teams to opposite sides of the room and have them make as many paper wads as they can in two minutes. After two minutes say: Now I want you to guard your own paper wads while you try to steal as many as you can from 'he other team. Ready? Go!

After a few minutes, stop the activity.

RESPONSE

Ask: How did it feel to make as many paper wads as you could? How did it feel to protect your pile while trying to steal from the other team's pile? How is this like the way we sometimes try to get more and more material things?

Say: It's easy to get caught up in always wanting more. It may be compact discs or clothes. What other things do you like to collect?

Write the ideas on newsprint. Then have a volunteer read aloud Hebrews 13:5. Ask: What does this passage say about our lifestyle of always getting more and more stuff? What other ways can we find contentment?

CLOSING

Close with a prayer similar to this one: Thanks, God, for _____. (Go around the group and have kids each say one thing they have a lot of.) Help us not to be greedy in wanting more things, but rather to be content with what we have. Amen. ■

Stick It Out!

■ **Theme:** Patience, perseverance
■ **Scripture:** James 1:12
■ **Overview:** Group members will practice patience and perseverance by trying to thread a needle.
■ **Preparation:** You'll need a needle with a tiny eye and a 12-inch thread for each person. You'll also need a Bible, a pincushion and a table.

EXPERIENCE

Distribute a needle and thread to everyone. Have kids try to thread their needles. Let those who thread their needles quickly cheer on those who are having trouble. Give the last person to thread his or her needle a big round of applause.

RESPONSE

Ask: How did you feel as you tried to thread your needle? How did you feel when you succeeded? How did you feel about the encouragement you got? Why were some people more successful than others?

Talk about how ordinary people who persevere are often more successful in life than very talented people who give up easily. Ask kids to name situations in their lives that call for perseverance. Invite volunteers to share experiences in which perseverance paid off.

CLOSING

Read aloud James 1:12. Gather everyone around a table with a pincushion on it. Have kids take turns sticking their needles into the pincushion and saying, "I commit to sticking it out when I feel like giving up." ■

Who's the Boss?

■ **Theme:** Self-control
■ **Scripture:** 1 Thessalonians 5:5-11
■ **Overview:** Group members will see that though each person is tempted in different ways, God can give us control over temptations.
■ **Preparation:** Find several pictures in magazines of things that students are likely to be tempted by, such as food, attractive members of the opposite sex, clothing and alcohol. Tape these pictures around the room with a blank sheet of paper beneath each one. Gather pencils, wastebaskets and a Bible.

EXPERIENCE

Have students look at the pictures around the room. Tell kids they may each vote five times for the pictures that are most tempting to them by marking X's on the papers under the pictures. They can vote all five times for one picture or spread their votes around. After everyone has voted, tally the votes and announce the "Top Tempters."

Discuss what makes these things tempting. Ask how kids felt as they looked at the pictures.

RESPONSE

Read aloud 1 Thessalonians 5:5-11. Ask: How do you think the temptations you face are like the ones the Thessalonians faced? How are they different? What is the tempter trying to accomplish by putting temptations in the way of believers? How can we hang on to our self-control? How does being in a group like this help?

CLOSING

Say: The scripture we read tells us to encourage each other and build each other up. How does encouragement affect our self-control?

Who's the Boss?

Form two or three groups. Give a wastebasket to each group. Have groups take the tempting pictures down from the walls and tear them up into the wastebaskets. Then have kids in groups put their arms around each other and say words of affirmation and encouragement to the people on their right and left. For example, someone might say, "I know you can stay in control and walk away from temptation." ■

What Do You See?

■ **Theme:** Self-image
■ **Scripture:** Psalm 139; Isaiah 43:1; 1 Corinthians 13:12
■ **Overview:** Group members will discover that God sees our hearts and loves us, no matter what.
■ **Preparation:** Gather Bibles, two mirrors and a bowl of soapy water.

EXPERIENCE

Take a mirror and cover it with a film of soapy water. Pass it around the group and have kids look at themselves. Ask: What do you see? When you look in the mirror, what thoughts and feelings do you have about yourself? How can those feelings distort your self-image the way this soapy mirror distorts your physical image? What distorts the image we have of other people?

RESPONSE

Pass around the soap-covered mirror again, then pass the clear mirror. Read aloud 1 Corinthians 13:12. Ask: What does God see when he looks at us? How can we learn to see ourselves as God sees us?

Tell kids you want them each to yell their names on the count of three. After the outburst read Isaiah 43:1 aloud. Say: God knows your name! God loves you.

CLOSING

Go around the circle having kids take turns reading aloud the verses of Psalm 139. When kids come to the words "me" or "I" have them each substitute their own name. Make this a prayer of thanksgiving to God! ■

Stressed Out!

■ **Theme:** Stress
■ **Scripture:** Exodus 20:8-11; Psalm 37:3-5; Matthew 6:25-34
■ **Overview:** Group members will learn how to control stress by following God's prescription for daily living.
■ **Preparation:** Gather a rope for Tug of War and Bibles.

EXPERIENCE

Have a volunteer grip the middle of the Tug of War rope. Ask the volunteer to share what he or she does in a typical week. Each time the volunteer names an activity, add a person to one end of the rope, alternating so there is an equal number of people on each side of the rope. Add yourself if necessary to even out the numbers. When everyone is attached to the rope, start a Tug of War. The task of the volunteer is to hang on and try to stay balanced.

RESPONSE

Ask the volunteer: How was this experience like what happens in real life? How do you react to being pulled in all directions by school, church, family, friends? How do you get control of your life?

Have three kids read aloud the scripture passages. Ask: What is God's prescription for getting control of our lives? Why is this important? What can you learn from these passages to help you reduce stress?

CLOSING

Have kids find partners. In their pairs, have kids each finish this sentence: "The next time I'm stressed out I'll..."

Close with prayer for God to help kids keep a healthy balance in their lives. ■

Poison—Beware!

~~~~~~

■ **Theme:** Substance abuse

■ **Scripture:** 1 Corinthians 6:19-20

■ **Overview:** Group members will discover the poisonous nature of nicotine and other drugs and discuss why they are not appropriate for the people of God.

■ **Preparation:** In a quart jar place two cups of warm water and the tobacco from two cigarettes (or one small cigar or two teaspoons of pipe tobacco). Seal the jar tightly and let this concoction sit in the sun for a couple of hours. (After the meeting, dispose of the mixture by pouring it around your flower bed. It's an excellent insecticide.) You'll need a Bible.

EXPERIENCE

Gather the group in a circle. Show the jar with the (now) brown liquid in it to the group. Remove the lid and invite them to smell it. Encourage kids to give verbal reactions.

Explain that what they are smelling is a drug called nicotine. It is a naturally occurring poison contained in tobacco plants, and its distinctive odor is why most wild animals will not go near tobacco. Their sense of smell tells them that it's poison and warns them off.

Replace the lid on the jar and set it aside.

RESPONSE

Ask: Since nicotine is a poison and since its smell warns us that it is not good for us, why do people use it? What about the narcotic effect it has on its users? Why do people want or need that momentary euphoric feeling nicotine gives? Is there some other feeling we could replace it with? Explain.

Read 1 Corinthians 6:19-20 aloud. Discuss why it's important for Christians to follow these instructions.

CLOSING

Close with a prayer asking God's help in keeping our bodies pure. ■

The Fear of Failure

■ **Theme:** Success, failure
■ **Scripture:** Exodus 3:15; 4:1-16
■ **Overview:** Kids will see how they react to trying something new.
■ **Preparation:** You'll need a blindfold for each person. Put the following items in separate bowls: prunes, herring, anchovies and horseradish. Make sure you have enough of each food for all the group members to sample. Keep the bowls hidden or covered so kids can't see what they contain. You'll also need a Bible.

EXPERIENCE

Have group members sit in a circle. Blindfold each person. Say: We're going to try something new. I'm going to pass around four bowls of different kinds of foods. I want you to put your fingers in each bowl and taste each food before passing it to the person on your right.

Ask kids not to give any verbal clues that would let other group members know what they've tasted.

RESPONSE

After everyone has tried (or refused) the food from all four bowls, have kids take off their blindfolds. Ask: How did you feel doing this taste test? Were you afraid or willing? Explain. How do you feel when someone forces you to try something new? How does it feel to try something new and fail? How does it feel to try something new and succeed?

Ask someone to read aloud Exodus 3:15; 4:1-16. Ask: Why did Moses make so many excuses? How did God help Moses deal with his fear of failure? How did he succeed in the end? What kinds of excuses do you make when someone asks you to try something new? What is God asking you to do that you're afraid to try?

The Fear of Failure

CLOSING

Have kids each find a partner. Say: Tell your partner one thing that you're going to try that you've always been afraid to try because you're afraid of failure. Then make a pact to either call each other during the week or pray for each other—whether you succeed or fail in the new thing. ■

Making Change

~~~~~~

■ **Theme:** Transitions
■ **Scripture:** Daniel 1:1-20; 2:48
■ **Overview:** Group members will be confused trying to sing different words to a familiar song, and will discuss the changes Daniel faced in Babylon.
■ **Preparation:** Gather 3×5 cards, pencils and a Bible.

EXPERIENCE

Have kids sing "Oh, When the Saints Go Marching In," but tell them they each have to make up their own words. No one is allowed to sing the words "oh," "when," "saints," "marching" or "in."

Rush right into the song—don't give kids time to think through what they're going to sing. Kids will likely have a tough time getting through the song and making up new words at the same time. Try it three or four times if necessary.

Ask: How did you feel trying to sing the song and make changes at the same time? How would it have been different if I'd given you the new words to sing? How were the feelings you had in the song like feelings you have when you face big changes or transitions in your life?

RESPONSE

Read aloud Daniel 1:1-20 and 2:48. Ask: What kind of transition did Daniel face in the first passage? How did Daniel handle that transition? What kind of results did he have?

Give kids each a 3×5 card and have them write on it a transition they'll be facing soon. Then say: Our attitudes have a lot to do with how we handle transitions. Below what you just wrote, write the kind of attitude that would help you through the transition you wrote about.

Let volunteers tell what they wrote.

Making Change

CLOSING

Ask: Who did Daniel rely on to help him through the changes he faced? How can we rely on God to get us through the changes we face?

Have kids pray silent or sentence prayers, asking God to help them through the transitions on their cards. Invite kids to give their cards to you to symbolize giving the transition to God. Use the cards to help you pray about the things your kids are facing. ■

10-Minute
Devotions on
Christ-Centered
Relationships

Oh Brother, Oh Sister!

■ **Theme:** Brothers and sisters

■ **Scripture:** Luke 10:38-42

■ **Overview:** Group members will create and act out a story that explores how siblings approach things differently.

■ **Preparation:** Gather a Bible, four pieces of paper and four pencils. Photocopy the "Tangled Story" handout and cut out each strip.

EXPERIENCE

Form four groups. (Groups don't need to have an equal number of people.) Give each group a piece of paper, a pencil and one strip from the "Tangled Story" handout. Have each group write a short paragraph that links the beginning sentence and ending sentences on its strip. Then have the groups plan how to act out what they've written.

When kids have finished writing, have groups take turns acting out their paragraphs.

Congratulate kids on their performances. Then ask: What was it like to hear all the parts of the story together? How did it add to the fun to have the different parts of the story from different perspectives? Do you ever feel like the kids in the story felt? Explain.

RESPONSE

Say: In the same way each team developed a different angle on the story, each person is unique. When we put stories together, it can be funny—and sometimes frustrating. That's how it sometimes is in families with brothers and sisters.

Have someone read Luke 10:38-42 aloud. Then ask: How was Martha feeling? What was wrong with her attitude? What could Martha learn from our tangled story? How are our actions toward our brothers and sisters similar to Martha's? What would Jesus say to us in situations such as the ones you acted out?

Oh Brother, Oh Sister!

CLOSING

Form a circle. Have kids sit, stand, kneel or choose whatever position they want. Then pray: God, help us see the unique talents our brothers and sisters have, and not expect others to act just like we do. Amen. ■

Tangled Story

----

1. Jim and John were brothers, but they were very different. Once they . . .

This caused them to get into a big fight.
----

2. Whenever Jim and John (who were brothers) got into a fight, they yelled at each other. The worst time was when . . .

Their sisters, Julie and Jane, said, "Why don't you guys just learn to work things out peacefully?"
----

3. Julie and Jane (who were sisters) managed to work out their differences even though their personalities were quite different. One day at school . . .

Julie and Jane gave each other a big hug.
----

4. Julie and Jane (who were sisters) really knew how to make each other feel appreciated and loved. They even . . .

Julie and Jane liked being sisters.

The Art of Compromise

■ **Theme:** Conflicts

■ **Scripture:** Genesis 13:1-9

■ **Overview:** Group members will play a game that highlights the benefits of using compromise to settle conflicts.

■ **Preparation:** Gather Bibles and four 3×5 cards, two with a blue dot and two with a red dot. You'll need a watch with a second hand or a stopwatch. Write the following scoring instructions on two sheets of paper:

1. Both teams play blue: 100 points each.
2. Both teams play red: -100 points each.
3. One teams plays blue, the other red: blue gets -100; red gets +100.

EXPERIENCE

Form two teams and have them stand on opposite sides of the room. Give each team a set of scoring instructions, a card with a red dot and a card with a blue dot.

Give these directions clearly but do not clarify anything else.

Say: We are going to play a game. The score sheet explains how to get points. I'll give you 15 seconds to decide which color card to play. Bring it to me when I call time. Don't let the other team know what color you're planning to play.

Play five rounds of the game using 15-second intervals for teams to decide which card to play. Announce the score after each round.

Bring the teams together. Ask: How could conflict have been avoided? (By both teams compromising and playing blue each time.) How did the desire to beat the other team create conflict? Why is the desire to win often so much stronger than the desire to keep peace?

RESPONSE

Read Genesis 13:1-9 together. Ask: What kind of conflict was going on between Lot and Abram? How was the conflict

The Art of Compromise

settled? What was good about the way Abram handled the situation? (He wanted to reach a compromise and settle the problem.)

Discuss when it's good to compromise and when compromising is inappropriate.

CLOSING

Ask students to share an area of their life where there is conflict. Let the group suggest ways compromise can be used to settle the conflicts. Close with prayer. ■

Family Tension

■ **Theme:** Family, parents
■ **Scripture:** Exodus 20:12
■ **Overview:** Teenagers will explore ways to ease the pain of separation from parents that is a natural part of growing up.
■ **Preparation:** You'll need a thin rubber band for each member of the group and a Bible.

EXPERIENCE

Gather the group in a circle and distribute rubber bands. Have kids each share their rubber band with the person to their right. Have group members gradually step back, stretching the rubber bands between them almost to the breaking point, but not quite. Have kids hold this position.

RESPONSE

Ask: What will happen if you continue to step apart? Which people are likely to get hurt when the rubber bands pop? How is this tension like the tension that naturally develops in families as teenagers grow more and more independent?

Say: As we grow older and more mature, we take more responsibility for our own lives. We gradually separate from our parents. If the separation isn't handled gently, it can cause pain for everyone involved.

Read Exodus 20:12 aloud. Have kids step forward and ease the tension on the rubber bands.

Ask: How does respecting our parents help ease the tension and pain of separation? Why do you think scripture places so much emphasis on respecting parents?

CLOSING

Close with prayer, asking God to help kids show respect for their parents as they work through the process of separation and progress toward adulthood. Have kids wear rubber bands on their wrists as a reminder. ■

Oops!

■ *Theme:* Forgiveness
■ *Scripture:* Matthew 18:21-22
■ *Overview:* Group members will decide how to be forgiving when a team member messes up.
■ *Preparation:* You'll need four buckets, four trays of ice cubes and treats for everyone in the group. You'll also need a Bible.

EXPERIENCE

Form two teams. Have each team stand single file. Put one bucket with ice cubes from two trays of ice in front of the first person in line for each team. Put a bucket between the legs of the last person in line.

Say: We're going to have a race to see which team can pass all the ice cubes in the front bucket back to the last person in line, who will drop the ice cubes into the second bucket.

Say: But there's a catch: You must never turn around—you can only look straight ahead. You'll pass the ice cubes one at a time over your back to the person behind you. If someone drops a cube, that person must pass the cube forward by giving it to the person in front of him or her through his or her legs. That ice cube must travel all the way to the first person who can then pass it back over his or her back.

Award the winning team a snack.

RESPONSE

Ask the losing team members: How did it feel to see your teammates drop the ice cubes? How did it feel to be the first person in line and not know what was going on behind you? Did you feel forgiving toward your teammates who messed up? Why or why not?

Now give members of the losing team their snack.

Ask: Now is it easier for you to forgive your teammates who messed up? Explain.

Oops!

Have a volunteer read aloud Matthew 18:21-22. Ask: Why is it sometimes hard to forgive others? What does this passage tell us about forgiveness?

CLOSING

Pick up one ice cube. Have the group form a circle. Have each group member pass the ice cube around the circle and say, "I promise to be a forgiving friend," as he or she passes the ice cube to the person to the right. ■

The Friendship Factor

■ **Theme:** Friendship
■ **Scripture:** Proverbs 18:24; John 15:14-15
■ **Overview:** Kids will discuss what makes a good friend and pick one "friendship factor" to work on themselves.
■ **Preparation:** You'll need balloons, a marker, newsprint, string and a Bible.

EXPERIENCE

Have the group quickly brainstorm "friendship factors" and list their ideas on newsprint. Have them vote on the five most important factors, then print each of the five on an inflated balloon. Have the group stand in a circle and bounce the five balloons among themselves, trying to keep them all in the air at once. (If you have more than 15 kids, make two sets of balloons and have kids do this activity in two groups.) If a balloon hits the floor, stop everything and discuss for a few seconds what a friend would be like without that quality. If the same balloon is dropped more than once, discuss what a friend would be like without one of the other friendship factors.

Read Proverbs 18:24 and John 15:14-15 aloud. Talk about the friendship factors in those verses. List them on newsprint and compare that list to the list kids made earlier.

RESPONSE

Ask kids each to choose the friendship factor that is most important to them. Ask why they like having friends who display those qualities. Then have kids each name one friendship factor they'd like to develop in their own lives.

CLOSING

Gather the balloons and use string to tie them into a balloon bouquet. Have kids help you hang the balloon bouquet from the ceiling. Say: Friends feel empty without other friends to keep them going, just as we kept these balloons going. Let's all work at being the kind of friend Jesus is to all of us. ■

Come Join Us!

■ **Theme:** Including others
■ **Scripture:** Galatians 3:26-28
■ **Overview:** Group members will learn to be sensitive to peers who may feel left out.
■ **Preparation:** You'll need a Bible.

EXPERIENCE

Ask for a volunteer and have that person leave the room. With the remaining kids, form two groups and ask the groups to go to opposite sides of the room.

Tell one group to form a close huddle facing inward and do everything it can to keep the volunteer out of the circle. Have the other group form a huddle facing outward and welcome the volunteer when he or she returns.

Before you bring the volunteer back into the room, tell him or her to try to get into both groups. After he or she successfully joins the outward-facing group, ask: How did it feel to be the person trying to get into these huddles? How did it feel to be in a team that wouldn't let the person in? How is the inward-facing group's attitudes like the attitudes we sometimes display toward others in real life?

RESPONSE

Read aloud Galatians 3:26-28, then ask: According to the passage, how should we treat each other? Why is it sometimes difficult to include others who are different? What can we do to act more like the outward-facing group? How can we be more sensitive to others who don't appear to fit in?

CLOSING

Have group members form a circle with their arms around each other's shoulders. Lead in prayer, asking God to help kids be more sensitive to others by including others in their circles instead of leaving them out. Close by singing "We Are His Hands" from *The Group Songbook* (Group Books). ■

Your Eyes Can Fool You

■ **Theme:** Judging
■ **Scripture:** Matthew 7:1-5
■ **Overview:** Kids will judge two different characters and decide how judging can be harmful.
■ **Preparation:** Photocopy the "Running for President" handout and cut out the two strips. You'll also need a Bible.

EXPERIENCE

Ask two volunteers to leave the room. Tell the rest of the group that two people running for president will be coming into the room. Each candidate will give a short speech listing his or her credentials. Afterward, everyone will vote for the best candidate.

Give each of the volunteers a slip of paper from the "Running for President" handout. Tell the volunteers each to read the list of credentials on their paper.

Have the two volunteers enter the room and give their speeches. Then have group members vote for the best candidate.

Then say: Both of these candidates represent actual people. The candidate with all the glowing credentials was Jim Jones, a cult-leader who died in Jonestown, Guyana, with more than 900 of his followers in a mass suicide. The other candidate was Jesus.

RESPONSE

Ask: What did you think of these two candidates before I told you who they were? How did you feel after I revealed their true identities? What does the outcome of this election tell us about the things we judge to be most important? What other priorities might we consider in evaluating people?

Read aloud Matthew 7:1-5, and ask: What happens when we judge someone too quickly? Why is it hard not to judge people? What does this passage challenge us to do in our relationships with others?

Your Eyes Can Fool You

CLOSING

Encourage kids to silently confess their tendency to judge others as you pray: God, forgive us for being judgmental. (Pause.) Help us take time to really get to know people. Amen. ■

Running for President

Candidate #1: "I created soup kitchens for the poor and counseled drug addicts. I have been involved in politics in California and was chairman of San Francisco's Housing Authority Commission. I won the Los Angeles Herald's Humanitarian of the Year Award. I'm an ordained minister."

Candidate #2: "I insult lawyers and church leaders. I've been arrested. I've never held an elected office. I don't own a home. Some people have called me a drunk; others say I'm possessed by the devil."

Everyone Wins!

■ **Theme:** Loving enemies
■ **Scripture:** Luke 6:32-36
■ **Overview:** Kids will experience helping an "enemy" win and will see how Jesus wants us to treat people who don't treat us kindly.
■ **Preparation:** Gather paper, pencils, a wastebasket and a Bible.

EXPERIENCE

Form pairs and pass out paper and pencils for Tick-Tack-Toe. But announce one variation: Both players should try to make the X's win. If the X's win, both partners win, even though one was marking O's.

Let partners play once; then have them switch letters and play again. Ask: How did it feel to help someone else win? How did it feel when both partners "won"? How is that different from the way you usually play Tick-Tack-Toe?

Have someone read aloud Luke 6:32-36. Then ask: How is what we just did in Tick-Tack-Toe like what Jesus wants us to do in real life?

RESPONSE

Ask: Who are our "enemies" in life?

Have partners use their Tick-Tack-Toe paper to list people they might consider enemies. Have partners give each other suggestions about how to show Jesus' love to those enemies.

CLOSING

Have partners tear their sheets in half and have each partner hold one half. One pair at a time, have kids wad up and toss their papers in a wastebasket as they say, "Because of God's love, we can show love to our enemies." ■

You Heard What?

■ **Theme:** Peace-making
■ **Scripture:** Romans 14:19
■ **Overview:** Kids will examine how they can respond to conflict in a peace-seeking way.
■ **Preparation:** Photocopy and cut apart enough slips from the "Making Peace" handout so that each group of three will have a set. You'll need a Bible for every three people.

EXPERIENCE

Form groups of three. Give each group a set of slips from the "Making Peace" handout. Be sure each person gets one slip and keeps what it says a secret from the other group members. If you don't have exactly three people in each group, have two people take the role of Person #3. Have groups role play their situations, following the directions on their slips.

Stop the role-plays before anyone gets violent, and ask: How did it feel trying to make peace in your group? How is this experience like trying to make peace between two people who are really angry with each other? How did it feel to be one of the people who were fighting?

RESPONSE

Say: Our natural response in many situations is to fight rather than to make peace. But let's see what Romans has to say about fighting and peace.

Have kids return to their groups of three and read Romans 14:19 together. Have groups each come up with responses that Person #1 and Person #2 could have made that might have led to peace. Encourage them to base their responses on the message of the passage.

Bring everyone together and have each group report its peace-making responses.

You Heard What?

CLOSING

Say: When we find ourselves in conflict with someone else, the best thing to do is to seek a solution that will make both people feel better.

Close with prayer, asking God to help kids act as peacemakers in conflicts. ■

Making Peace

Photocopy and cut apart a set of slips for each group of three.

Person #1

You've just found out that a kid at school said you're a lousy basketball player and the only reason you made the team is because your mom is a teacher. That accusation makes you furious. When you meet the person in the hall after school you say, "I understand you don't think I should have made the team."

Person #2

You're upset because a kid you don't think is very good made the basketball team and you didn't. You told some friends that the kid only made the team because he or she is a teacher's kid. You're angry about not making the team, and you're ready to defend your position when you meet the kid in the hall after school. You're mad enough to fight.

Person #3

You're walking down the hall after school when you see two of your friends in a heated discussion. You decide to help them make peace. Do all you can to get them settled down.

Choosing Teams

■ **Theme:** Peer influence
■ **Scripture:** Romans 12:2
■ **Overview:** Group members will examine how peer influences affect their decisions.
■ **Preparation:** Place a few cookie cutters and a cross in a paper bag. You'll also need a Bible.

EXPERIENCE

Ask three volunteers to leave the room. Have the rest of the students form two teams and sit in opposite corners of the room. Explain that both teams are to try to get the volunteers to join them and sit in their corner. However, team members are not allowed to leave their seats or tell the volunteers why they want them to join their side.

Have the volunteers return to the room one by one, and instruct them to be seated.

RESPONSE

Read aloud Romans 12:2. Ask the volunteers: How did you feel when you had to decide which group to join? How was this like the pressure you feel in real life when different people try to influence your decisions? How do you decide what to do? In what ways does the world try to influence Christians to "join the team"?

Next, brainstorm ideas to help Christians resist the temptation to conform to the world's standards.

CLOSING

Take the cookie cutters from the bag. Tell kids that the world wants to shape them to fit its mold. Then take out the cross. Explain that by following Christ we can break free from the "moldy" influences of our peers and our world. Then instead of being conformers, we can become transformers. Pray for God's help to do just that. ■

5-Minute Servants

■ **Theme:** Servanthood
■ **Scripture:** Romans 7:6
■ **Overview:** Group members will look for ways to serve and discuss the biblical motivation for serving.
■ **Preparation:** Gather cleaning supplies such as paper towels, brooms, buckets, spray cleaner and sponges. You'll also need a whistle, newsprint, a marker and a Bible.

EXPERIENCE

Gather everyone in a circle with the cleaning supplies on the floor in the center. Ask group members to think about the last time they voluntarily did a servant task at home, at school or for a neighbor, without expecting payment and without being asked. After several kids have responded, tell the group that they will be on a service mission for the next five minutes.

When you say "go," kids are to take a cleaning tool from the center of the circle and spend five minutes using that tool as a servant someplace close by. Explain that you'll blow a whistle when time is up.

RESPONSE

When kids return, ask them to list all the things they did in the five minutes. Jot their responses on newsprint. Praise the group for all they accomplished in such a short time. Ask: How did you feel during your five minutes of service? How does looking at this list make you feel? What made this service opportunity more fun than some others? What could you do to make other service opportunities more enjoyable?

CLOSING

Have someone read Romans 7:6 aloud. Ask: What does God want our motive for service to be? What effects do our motives have on the work we do?

Close with prayer, asking God to help kids be sensitive to service opportunities and to serve with the right motives. ■

Timing Is Everything

■ **Theme:** Sexuality
■ **Scripture:** Ecclesiastes 3:1; 1 Thessalonians 4:3-8
■ **Overview:** Students will discover the wisdom of waiting and apply it to their own sexual conduct.
■ **Preparation:** You'll need a copy of your favorite cookie recipe and the utensils and ingredients to make them. You'll also need Bibles. You may choose to get access to an oven and have the group finish making the cookies after the devotion.

EXPERIENCE

Set out the cookie recipe, the necessary ingredients and utensils. Have group members choose kids to fill the roles of measurer, stirrer and eater. Say: You're in a race against time to get these cookies mixed. Hurry, but be as accurate as you can. I'll tell you when time is up.

Call time after a few ingredients are mixed, but while the mixture is still pretty disgusting to eat. Ask the eater to try the mixture and report on the taste. Say: I know that we didn't have time to get everything in place, but, hey, we have everything we need to make cookies, right? (Pause) Actually, we don't. We need more time to do it right.

RESPONSE

Have someone read Ecclesiastes 3:1 and 1 Thessalonians 4:3-8 aloud. Say: God has equipped us all to be sexual beings, but just because all the ingredients are there doesn't mean the timing is right.

Ask why God has so many guidelines for sexual conduct. Have the group discuss advantages of saving sex for marriage. Say: It isn't that God never wants you to have sex. But for your own protection he wants you to wait for the right time—marriage—and the right person—your spouse. God has made his rules very plain, and those who choose to break them often end up paying a heavy price.

Timing Is Everything

CLOSING

Go back to the cookie ingredients. Say: These cookies are my favorite. I can tell you from experience that the right ingredients and the right timing make a huge difference in how they turn out. God knows better than anyone how relationships work. We can trust his guidance that there's wisdom in waiting. ■

Too Good to Keep

■ **Theme:** Witnessing, sharing faith
■ **Scripture:** Acts 4:18-20
■ **Overview:** Group members will experience one member sharing food with the rest and compare that to sharing the good news with others.
■ **Preparation:** Bring an appetizing treat, such as a beautifully decorated cake or a still-warm pizza. You'll also need slips of paper, pencils, an old hat and a Bible.

EXPERIENCE

As kids arrive, have them each write their name on a slip of paper and drop it into a hat. Then have everyone sit in a circle. Display the food you brought. Say: Some lucky individual is going to win this entire (name the food). I'm going to draw a name from the hat. The person whose name I draw gets the whole banana.

Have kids do a drum roll on their knees as you make a big production of drawing the name out of the hat. Place the food in the winning person's lap. Then take a seat in the circle and stare expectantly at the winner, cuing the rest of the group to do the same. When the winner offers to share the food, give him or her a big round of applause. (If the winner never offers to share, whisper loudly in his or her ear that it's time to share the food.)

RESPONSE

As everyone eats, ask the group: How did it feel *not* to be the winner? What were you hoping would happen? How would you have felt if (name) had never shared the food?

Ask the winner: How did it feel to be the winner? How did it feel to have everyone staring expectantly? What made you decide to share the food?

Read aloud Acts 4:18-20. Ask: How was Peter and John's telling about Jesus like (name) sharing the food with us? What was their motive for sharing? How would keeping all the food be like not sharing the good news about Jesus?

Too Good to Keep

CLOSING

Say: Some things are just too good to be kept to ourselves. Look for ways you can share the good news this week. ■

10-Minute Devotions on Faith Issues

Get an Attitude

■ **Theme:** Church
■ **Scripture:** Psalm 42:4; 122:1
■ **Overview:** Group members will express their feelings about attending church.
■ **Preparation:** Prepare a list of about 20 places kids in your group might go, such as school, a shopping mall or the movies. Be sure to include church on your list. You will also need a Bible.

EXPERIENCE

Ask the group to respond to each of the statements you're about to read with cheers, boos, hisses or other exclamations that express their feelings about your statement. Then read your list of places, saying: "Today you're going to the orthodontist"; "Today you're going to Disneyland"; and so on. After each statement pause for kids' responses.

Ask: What determines your feelings about going to a certain place? Is it related to fun? boredom? who will be there?

RESPONSE

Have volunteers read Psalm 42:4 and Psalm 122:1 aloud. Then ask: How did the Psalmist feel about going to worship God? Why do you think he felt this way? What are your feelings about church? How do your feelings affect your friends? your family? How do you think God would like us to feel as we prepare to come to his house? If our attitudes need improving, what specific things can we do to help them?

CLOSING

Bring everyone together in a circle. Ask kids to pray sentence prayers thanking God for things or people they are thankful for at your church. ■

Believe It or Not!

■ **Theme:** Doubts

■ **Scripture:** Matthew 14:22-33; John 20:24-29

■ **Overview:** From scriptures about the disciples, group members will discover that doubt is a natural part of the faith process.

■ **Preparation:** Gather a large paper sack, a 3×5 card and a pencil for each person. You'll also need a Bible and an offering plate.

EXPERIENCE

Have everyone sit on the floor. Instruct kids to put their hands on their heads with their elbows tucked in close to their faces. Place a paper bag over the head, hands and upper body of each group member.

Ask: What do you see? How do you feel? How is being in the sack like doubting God? How does doubt feel?

Have kids use their fingers to tear peep holes in their sacks. Ask: What can you see now? What helps you get past your doubts?

Have kids break out of their sacks. Ask: How does it feel to get out of your sack? What helps you break through the times of doubt in your life?

RESPONSE

Have volunteers read aloud the two scripture passages. Ask: Why did the disciples doubt? How did they overcome their doubt? What things in our lives cause us to experience doubt? What can we learn from these passages about overcoming doubt? What has helped you overcome doubt in your own lives?

Assure the group that doubt is a normal part of our faith journey. Say: Even the disciples—Jesus' closest friends and followers—experienced doubts from time to time. But they kept looking to God until he gave the answers they needed.

Believe It or Not!

CLOSING

Distribute pencils and 3×5 cards. Have kids each jot down their most troubling doubt. Pass around an offering plate and collect the cards as a symbol of offering kids' doubts to God. Close with prayer, asking God to help kids through their times of doubt. ■

Stompin' Stewards

■ **Theme:** Earth, creation
■ **Scripture:** Genesis 2:15
■ **Overview:** Group members will be reminded of what it means to be caretakers of God's creation.
■ **Preparation:** Gather five empty, uncrushed, recyclable soft drink cans for each group member. You'll also need tape, newsprint, markers and a Bible.

EXPERIENCE

Tape several sheets of newsprint to the wall. Distribute markers and ask group members each to find a place to list everything they've used during the day—from toothpaste and toilet paper to food, clothing and electricity. When the lists are complete, have kids go back and mark a big R by the items that can be recycled or "renewed" in some way. Have them mark a C by items that have simply been consumed. Then have kids each count up the number of R's and C's on their list and report the results to the group.

RESPONSE

Have a volunteer read Genesis 2:15 aloud. Ask: What does this Bible passage say about the way we use the Earth's resources? How many people are satisfied with their R-to-C ratio? What can we do to improve it?

Talk about your stewardship of God's resources in your group activities and what you can do to become better stewards.

CLOSING

Gather everyone in a circle. Place five empty soft drink cans on the floor in front of each person. Ask kids to respond to each line of the closing litany by repeating the words "We thank you, Lord!" and stomping a can. Read the following responsive prayer:

Stompin' Stewards

For your Earth—the light, the dark and the energy it produces—
> We thank you, Lord! (can crush)

For the birds of the air and the fish in the sea—
> We thank you, Lord! (can crush)

For the animals that provide food and clothing for us—
> We thank you, Lord! (can crush)

For the people who inhabit the Earth, family and friends—
> We thank you, Lord! (can crush)

For all the blessings you give to us day by day!
> We thank you, Lord! (can crush) ■

It Hurts to Say Goodbye

■ **Theme:** Grief
■ **Scripture:** 2 Samuel 1:17-27
■ **Overview:** Group members will imagine a loss and discuss the pain of saying goodbye.
■ **Preparation:** You'll need a sheet-cake pan, sand to fill the pan, a short candle for each group member, matches and a Bible. Optional: Have Linda Ronstadt's recording of the song "Goodbye My Friend."

EXPERIENCE

Dim the lights in your room. As group members arrive, give them each a candle. Have the pan filled with sand in front of the room with matches nearby.

Say: This candle represents the most important person or thing in your life. Think for a while what that person or thing is. Once you've decided, walk to the tray of sand, light your candle and set it in the tray. Remember where your candle is and watch it carefully.

After everyone has done this, pause so that everyone can see the tray filled with burning candles. Then say: Suppose the person represented by the candle died or the most important thing in your life was stolen.

Blow out all the candles to symbolize the loss and sit in darkness for a minute. If you were able to obtain Linda Ronstadt's recording of the song "Goodbye My Friend," play it now. Be ready to comfort young people for whom the experience may be particularly difficult. After the silence, ask: What have you been thinking about as we sat in silent darkness? What is hardest about the experience? What other times have you experienced similar feelings?

RESPONSE

Read aloud 2 Samuel 1:17-27. Ask: How did David feel? How did he express those feelings? How are his feelings similar to and different from your feelings after we blew out the

It Hurts to Say Goodbye

candles? How can knowing about David's feelings of sadness help you express your own sadness in tough times?

CLOSING

Have kids pair off, face their partners and hold hands. Read aloud each line of this prayer and ask kids to repeat it.

God, sometimes we feel sad when we lose someone or something that's important to us.

Help us realize that it's okay to feel sad.

Help us express our feelings to others and to you.

Thank you for the love and comfort you give us

and for caring friends who support and help us.

Amen. ■

Aiming for Hope

■ **Theme:** Hope
■ **Scripture:** Romans 5:1-5
■ **Overview:** Group members will see that hope is worth having despite apparent circumstances.
■ **Preparation:** You'll need an empty soft drink bottle, a bucket, two opaque pitchers filled with water and one opaque pitcher filled with confetti or shredded newspaper. You'll also need a Bible.

EXPERIENCE

Ask for two assistants. Place the empty soft drink bottle in a bucket. Have the two assistants take turns standing on a chair and attempt to pour water from their pitchers into the soft drink bottle below.

Now ask for a volunteer—preferably one with a reputation for spending a lot of time on personal appearance—to sit in a chair. Have one assistant hold the soft drink bottle over the head of the volunteer. Encourage the volunteer to look up. Stand on a chair over the volunteer and explain that even through you haven't practiced, you want to be the one to fill the bottle this time. Stop and ask the kids what possible hope the volunteer has in this situation. After kids respond, make a show of pouring your confetti-filled pitcher over the volunteer.

Ask someone to read aloud Romans 5:1-5. Talk about how tough situations can teach us to have hope. Say: Each time God helps us through a problem, we learn to trust him more. Then it's easier to believe that he'll take care of the next tough thing that comes our way.

RESPONSE

Ask the volunteer how it felt right before he or she was "doused" with confetti. Ask kids to tell what gives them hope in tough times.

Aiming for Hope

CLOSING

Say: When we face a tough situation, it's hard to see the complete picture. God has options we've never even thought of. Placing our trust in him gives us hope.

Close with a prayer of thanks for the way God works things out in our lives. ■

Finding the Balance

- **Theme:** Justice, mercy
- **Scripture:** Micah 6:8
- **Overview:** Group members will reflect on the importance of balancing justice with mercy.
- **Preparation:** You'll need a Bible and three different-colored sheets of paper. Cut the paper into four pieces each, so you have 12 rectangles.

On each of four rectangles of one color write one of these statements: "Give a hug." "Say 'I love you.'" "Be extra positive and encouraging." "Give a pat on the shoulder." (These are the mercy/kindness cards.)

On the rectangles of the second color write: "You're grounded." "No allowance for a week." "No car for a month." "No television until you bring your grades up." (These are the justice cards.)

On the rectangles of the third color write: "I took the car without your permission." "I came home 30 minutes after curfew." "I was caught shoplifting a CD." "I'm failing two subjects at school." (These are the problem cards.)

Place four chairs against one wall. Set up a table a few feet in front of the chairs.

EXPERIENCE

As kids come in, single out four of them, hand them each a problem card and have them sit in the chairs by the wall. Explain to the rest of the group that these are the problem kids.

Have each problem kid stand and read his or her card. Spread the mercy/kindness cards and the justice cards out on the table. Read Micah 6:8 aloud. Say: The rest of you are a parent group. You're going to try to put Micah's advice into practice by choosing both a mercy/kindness card and a justice card for each offense.

Have the problem children stand one by one and read their offenses again. Have the parent group work together to choose appropriate responses.

Finding the Balance

RESPONSE

After all four problem children have been given responses, ask: How did you feel about making these decisions? What would you have done differently? How did you problem children feel about the responses you were given? Why is it important to combine justice and mercy, instead of applying just one or the other?

CLOSING

Read Micah 6:8 again. Say: God is both a God of justice and a God of mercy. He wants us, as his followers, to reflect both those qualities in our lives as well.

Close with a prayer for guidance in our relationships with others. ■

Risky Business

■ **Theme:** Love

■ **Scripture:** John 15:13-14; Romans 5:8

■ **Overview:** Group members will decide what they're willing to risk for the things and people they love.

■ **Preparation:** Make a list of things kids would be willing to take risks for. Include both big-risk and small-risk items such as a friend, an enemy, a car, a sibling, good health, a good grade in school and a tuna fish sandwich. Make four signs indicating what kids would be willing to risk for the items on the list. Write one of the following phrases on each sign: "My Life," "My Reputation," "My Savings" and "My Third Cousin's Pet Hamster." You'll also need Bibles.

EXPERIENCE

Place one of the signs on each wall. Read from your list of items, and have kids stand by the sign that represents the highest risk they would take for each item. For example, a student might risk his life for a friend but only his third cousin's hamster for a tuna sandwich. After you've gone through your list, bring everyone together.

RESPONSE

Say: The things you are willing to risk the most for are the things that you love the most. Do you agree or disagree?

Then have volunteers read John 15:13-14 and Romans 5:8. Say: What Jesus loves most is people. What did he risk for us? What are we willing to risk for him?

CLOSING

Close by having the group read Romans 5:8 in unison. Then say: Jesus showed his love by dying for us. Let's show our love by living for him! ■

Haves and Have Nots

■ **Theme:** Missions
■ **Scripture:** Matthew 28:18-20; James 2:14-17
■ **Overview:** Group members will experience being "haves" or "have nots."
■ **Preparation:** Bring a snack for everyone in the group. You'll also need a Bible.

EXPERIENCE

Form two groups. Have one group sit in a circle in the center of the room. Have the other group split up and go to the four corners of the room. Distribute snacks to the middle group only. Sit down, chat and eat with them as the groups in the corners watch. Then bring everyone together.

RESPONSE

Discuss with the middle group how it felt to be eating while the other group looked on. Discuss with the corner group how they felt about being excluded from the food and conversation. Ask: How was the relationship between the two groups like the relationship between Christians in the United States and people in third-world countries?

Have someone read aloud Matthew 28:18-20 and James 2:14-17. Have the kids in the middle group distribute snacks to the group that had been in the corners. Ask: What is our responsibility toward people who don't know Jesus? toward people who lack food and material things? What can we do as a group to fulfill that responsibility?

CLOSING

Have kids vote on one thing to do as a group in response to Jesus' command. Close with sentence prayers for the needy people of the world. ■

Slow Down

■ **Theme:** Rest
■ **Scripture:** Matthew 14:22-23
■ **Overview:** Kids will experience what it's like not to rest and decide how they'll take time to rest this week.
■ **Preparation:** Have a piece of paper and pencil for each group member. You'll also need a Bible.

EXPERIENCE

Lead the group in five minutes of non-stop calisthenics. Don't let anyone rest. Shout out exercises such as jogging in place, 25 sit-ups, 15 push-ups, 30 jumping jacks, jogging around the room twice. Continue shouting out different strenuous exercises until five minutes are up and kids are obviously tired.

RESPONSE

As group members rest, ask: How did it feel to do strenuous exercise without stopping? What would happen if I had you do these exercises for one hour straight? Why is it important to rest?

Ask someone to read aloud Matthew 14:22-23. Then ask: What did Jesus do in these two passages? Why? How important is it to rest? How can we rest our minds as well as our bodies? Why do we sometimes push ourselves instead of taking time to rest? How do you rest and relax?

CLOSING

Give kids each a piece of paper and pencil. Have them write one way they'll rest both their bodies and minds this week.

Form groups of three. Have kids each tell their group how they plan to make time to rest this week. Then have the groups close in prayer, asking for God's help in making time to rest and relax. ■

I'm Clean!

■ **Theme:** Sin, forgiveness
■ **Scripture:** Romans 3:23 and 2 Corinthians 5:21
■ **Overview:** Kids will experience the effects of sin and the power of God's forgiveness.
■ **Preparation:** You'll need newspaper; a damp, white towel; and a Bible.

EXPERIENCE

Have kids form pairs. Give each pair a section of newspaper. Have one partner hold the newspaper on the floor while the other partner drags his or her hands across it, palms down. Then have partners switch roles.

Ask kids to look at their hands. Ask: How is staining your hands with ink like getting involved with sin?

Read aloud Romans 3:23. Ask: How do you feel as you look at your sin-stained hands? How is the ink on your hands like or unlike sin's real effects on us?

RESPONSE

Read aloud 2 Corinthians 5:21. Say: This towel represents Jesus. As Jesus comes to you, wipe sin's effects on Jesus— remembering that he died to take away your sins.

Pass the damp, white towel to all group members and have them each wipe their hands clean.

CLOSING

Take the towel and hold it up so everyone can see the dark smudges on it. Pray: Thank you, Jesus, for dying for our sins. Thank you for loving us and forgiving us. In Jesus' name, amen. ■

Use It or Lose It

■ **Theme:** Stewardship

■ **Scripture:** Psalm 24:1; Matthew 25:14-30

■ **Overview:** Group members will experience "active stewardship" and commit to being active during the upcoming week with one talent God has given them.

■ **Preparation:** You'll need a Bible and enough modeling clay for four small groups.

EXPERIENCE

Form four groups. Distribute the clay among them. Say: This clay is mine, but I'm loaning it to you for a few minutes. You can do anything with it. Make your decision as a group and act on it.

After a few minutes bring everyone together and have groups tell what they decided to do with their clay and why.

RESPONSE

Say: People react differently to opportunities. Let's see how God looks at opportunities.

Ask someone to read the scripture passages aloud. Discuss God's perspective on what he has given his people and how they should respond.

CLOSING

Take each group's clay and put it on your desk or a table where everyone can see it. Point to one or more examples of clay that was formed into something. Say: God gives each of us talents, abilities and resources he expects us to use and develop for him. Think of one thing God has gifted you with and make a commitment to invest it in his kingdom during the coming week.

Close with prayer, asking God to bless kids as they use their gifts for God's glory. ■

Hide 'n' Seek

■ **Theme:** Time With God
■ **Scripture:** Jeremiah 29:11-13
■ **Overview:** Kids will search for valuable possessions and realize that God is valuable and worth searching for regularly.
■ **Preparation:** You'll need a Bible.

EXPERIENCE

Form pairs. Have partners find the most valuable possession they have on or with them, such as a piece of jewelry or a picture of someone special. Ask partners to trade valuable possessions. Encourage kids to treat the traded items with respect and care.

Have one partner close his or her eyes while the other partner hides the traded item. Then have partners switch roles. After both items are hidden, have partners try to find their valuable possessions in less than two minutes. If kids don't find their possessions, have their partners retrieve them.

RESPONSE

Afterward, ask: How did you feel as you looked for your possession? How did you feel when you found your possession? when you didn't?

Say: You may or may not have found your valuable possession, but God promises that if you look, you'll find the most valuable possession you have: a relationship with him.

Read aloud Jeremiah 29:11-13. Ask: What do these verses reveal about God's desire for you to know him? What does it mean to search for God with your whole heart?

CLOSING

Ask kids to return to their partners and each make a commitment to spend time with God. Kids may wish to name a certain time each day or a certain number of times each week. After partners share their commitments, have them pray together to honor the commitments they've made. ■

Look Ahead

■ **Theme:** Vocation, future
■ **Scripture:** 1 Corinthians 12:4-11; Ephesians 4:7-16
■ **Overview:** Group members will explore their special gifts and think about making career decisions.
■ **Preparation:** Gather markers, a Bible and several sheets of gummed labels. You will also need an unshelled peanut for each person.

EXPERIENCE

Give kids each two gummed labels and a marker and have them write on each label one thing they like to do. Then have everyone stick their labels on their arms. Have kids take turns sharing what they like to do and why.

Appoint a scribe and give that person more gummed labels. Go around the group again. This time ask the group to name two things they think each person is particularly good at. The scribe will write those things on labels and give the labels to group members to stick on the person's arms. Have kids tell why they think each person is gifted in the areas they've named.

RESPONSE

Say: All gifts are given by God. That means all gifts are special, whether you have the gift of being a basketball star or the gift of being a loyal friend. There are lots of gifts, and they're all different!

Have volunteers read aloud the two scripture passages. Then ask: How does God want us to use our gifts? When and why do we tend to hide our gifts? How can thinking about our gifts be helpful as we make career choices?

CLOSING

Distribute peanuts and have kids open them. Ask: How is discovering our gifts like opening a peanut?

Look Ahead

Say: Sometimes it's hard to recognize our own gifts. We feel ordinary—kind of like this peanut—simple, and wrapped in a plain brown shell. It's not until you break open a peanut that you discover something is hidden inside. It's like that with people too. We need to break open our shells and discover the gifts we have inside.

Close with a circle prayer, having each person thank God for the gifts of the person on his or her left. ■

10-Minute
Devotions for
Special Occasions

New Year, New You

■ **Theme:** New Year's Day
■ **Scripture:** 2 Corinthians 5:17
■ **Overview:** Kids will see how something old and worthless can become new and worthwhile.
■ **Preparation:** Collect things out of the garbage, such as egg cartons, empty cans, empty cardboard boxes and empty plastic containers. Rinse the items and spread them out on a table. Gather tempera paint, paintbrushes, glue, construction paper, markers and a Bible.

EXPERIENCE

Form groups of three. Point out the "garbage table" and the art supplies. Say: Work together in your groups to create something new and wonderful out of this garbage. You have five minutes, starting now.

RESPONSE

After everyone has finished, ask: How did you feel about having to make something out of garbage? What do you think of your garbage now? What did you learn from this experience?

Say: When a new year starts, we often look at the icky things in our lives and resolve to improve them. Think about one of the things you want to improve.

Ask someone to read aloud 2 Corinthians 5:17. Then say: Just as you transformed this garbage into something neat, God can help you transform some of your bad habits into good ones. He can make you a new creation—a new you for the new year.

Ask: How does this passage challenge you as you look at a new year? How does it comfort you?

New Year, New You

CLOSING

Have group members sit in a circle and set their garbage creations in front of them. Go around the circle and have each person tell one thing he or she would like to transform in the coming year. Then close with prayer, thanking God for his power to transform. ■

Living Valentines

■ **Theme:** Valentine's Day
■ **Scripture:** 1 John 3:16-18; 4:19-21
■ **Overview:** Young people will make themselves into living valentines and commit to showing love for others in practical ways during the upcoming week.
■ **Preparation:** You'll need construction paper, markers, scissors, tape, valentine stickers and decorations, an instant camera and a Bible.

EXPERIENCE

Have kids form pairs and decorate each other as living valentines to be given to parents, family, a best friend or the other kids in the group. Then have kids take turns displaying their decorations to the whole group.

Have someone read 1 John 3:16-18 and 1 John 4:19-21. Say: Here we are, a bunch of living valentines. What is love all about, according to what we've just heard?

Give kids a few moments for discussion.

RESPONSE

Have members of the group discuss practical ways they can be valentines at home, at school, at church and among their friends. Encourage each student to choose one relationship that needs work and decide on one action he or she can take during the upcoming week to be a living valentine in that relationship.

CLOSING

Take a snapshot of each decorated student. Have kids take their snapshots home as reminders of the actions they'll be taking as living valentines during the upcoming week. Close in a group prayer. ■

Washed Clean

■ **Theme:** Lent
■ **Scripture:** Matthew 27:11-26; Hebrews 10:22-23
■ **Overview:** Group members will experience the "dirt" of sin.
■ **Preparation:** Mix dirt and water in a bucket to make thick mud. Arrange for the group to meet outdoors where there is a water faucet nearby. Gather a Bible and a roll of white paper towels.

EXPERIENCE

As kids gather, remind them that they are in the season of Lent, a time when Christians remember how sins can "dirty" their lives. Ask everyone to gather around the bucket, dip both hands into the mud, then sit down on the grass.

Have kids sit quietly as you read Matthew 27:11-26. (As the scripture passage is being read, the mud will begin to dry and become uncomfortable on the kids' hands.) After the reading, ask kids to describe what the drying mud feels like on their hands. Ask what it would feel like to join hands with others in the group. Discuss how the mud on kids' hands is like sin in their lives.

RESPONSE

As a group move toward the water faucet. Have kids take turns rinsing their hands. Hand kids each a paper towel and tell them each to dry the hands of another person in the group.

CLOSING

Have group members join hands as you read Hebrews 10:22-23 aloud. ■

Egg-ceptional Surprise!

■ **Theme:** Easter

■ **Scripture:** Mark 16:1-8

■ **Overview:** Group members will experience a surprise to remind them of the surprise that followed the death of Jesus.

■ **Preparation:** Hard boil and cool one egg for every two group members. Place the eggs back in the cartons so it appears that they're still raw. You'll also need a Bible.

EXPERIENCE

Form pairs. Give one member of each pair what appears to be a raw egg. Ask kids to go outside for an egg toss. Start with the pairs in two lines with partners facing each other. Ask them to toss the eggs back and forth to each other, moving one step backward after each toss. Typically, kids will get nervous as partners step further apart. (Only you know that the eggs are hard-boiled and won't break.) Keep the egg toss going until several pairs drop their eggs. Then bring everyone together.

RESPONSE

Ask how kids felt about tossing the eggs and how their feelings changed when they discovered the eggs were hard-boiled. Then read Mark 16:1-8 aloud. Ask: How are these eggs like the tomb that held Jesus' body?

Say: One reason eggs symbolize Easter is their similarity to the tomb. They're both completely sealed in and hard to get out of. And they both contain surprises! You probably expected raw eggs. Jesus' followers expected to find his body. Surprise—he had risen!

CLOSING

Close by reading this prayer: Lord, thank you for surprising us—with eggs, with friends, with your love and with your resurrection. Keep us always in your care. Amen.

Unless you have egg-lovers in the group, you may want to collect the eggs and make an egg-salad sandwich for yourself tomorrow! ■

Bringing Joy to Parents

- **Theme:** Mother's Day, Father's Day
- **Scripture:** Ephesians 6:1-3
- **Overview:** Group members will think about how hurtful, disrespectful words damage their relationships with parents, then prepare notes of affirmation.
- **Preparation:** Gather uninflated balloons, straight pins, self-stick notes and markers. You'll also need a Bible.

EXPERIENCE

As kids arrive, give them each a straight pin and an uninflated balloon. Gather everyone in a circle. Ask kids to tell some of the disrespectful or hurtful things they sometimes say to their parents. Have kids each poke a hole in their balloon each time a person shares a hurtful statement. After everyone has contributed to the discussion, ask kids to try to blow up their balloons.

Ask: Do you have a chance in the world of blowing up your balloons? Why not? How do hurtful words affect a relationship? How is saying hurtful things to your parents like poking pinholes in a balloon?

RESPONSE

Read Ephesians 6:1-3. Ask students to share ways they can show respect and honor to their parents. Discuss why Jesus wants them to love and obey their moms and dads.

Distribute self-stick notes and markers. Have kids write notes of affirmation and love on the self-stick notes. For example, one note might say: "Have a great day, Mom/Dad. I love you."

Encourage each person to write at least three notes to one or both parents. Explain that they are to take their notes home and place them around the house on Mother's or Father's Day as a way of showing respect and love.

Bringing Joy to Parents

CLOSING

Sit in a circle and ask each person to share one of his or her self-stick notes for each parent. Close with prayer, asking God's help in keeping hurtful words from harming relationships with parents. ■

To Win the Prize

■ **Theme:** Graduation
■ **Scripture:** Philippians 3:13-14
■ **Overview:** Kids will feel what it's like to be hindered in reaching a goal and discover what their response should be to reaching goals.
■ **Preparation:** Gather a hunk of modeling clay or Play-Doh for each group member. You'll also need Bibles.

EXPERIENCE

Distribute a hunk of modeling clay or Play-Doh to each group member. Tell kids each to think about what they'd like to become someday, then use the clay to create something that represents their goal. For example, if someone wants to be an electrician, he or she might make a long piece of wire from the clay.

As kids are working, go around and damage their creations. You can pretend to do it accidentally or intentionally. Before kids have a chance to make repairs, have them show their symbols. Then ask: How did it feel when I messed up what you were doing? What did you do? How is that experience like having people or circumstances prevent us from getting or doing exactly what we want?

Have kids read Philippians 3:13-14. Ask: How is your persistence in making your creations like what Paul says we should do? How does this passage relate to graduation?

RESPONSE

Read Philippians 3:13-14 aloud again. Then instruct kids to make something new with their clay, something that represents the prize they are striving to achieve as Christians. Have kids show and explain their new creations.

To Win the Prize

CLOSING

Say: Graduation is a big thing in any person's life. But there's a much bigger, more important goal for us to be striving for. And God is there to help us, if we depend on him.

Have kids pray for your graduates, asking God to help them keep their minds set on serving him and seeking the prize Paul wrote about in Philippians 3:13-14. ■

R & R

■ **Theme:** Summer vacation
■ **Scripture:** Mark 2:27; Hebrews 4:1-11
■ **Overview:** Students will discover that it's possible to do two things at once: be on vacation and think about God.
■ **Preparation:** You'll need bubble gum for one-third of the kids and kazoos for another third. You'll also need a Bible.

EXPERIENCE

Form three groups. Distribute bubble gum to one group and kazoos to another. Say: On my signal, the bubble gum group will start walking and chewing their gum at the same time. The kazoo group will start humming a popular song of their choice on the kazoos while pounding out the beat on their knees. The third group will start patting their heads and rubbing their stomachs at the same time.

Call time after about two minutes. **Ask:** How did you feel trying to do two things at the same time? Why were some things easier to do than others? What situations in real life call for you to do two things at once?

Ask volunteers to read aloud Mark 2:27 and Hebrews 4:1-11. Talk about how kids can enjoy rest and still recognize God in their lives.

RESPONSE

Have kids brainstorm ways they could think about God and honor him during summer vacation. Have kids each talk about one of their summer activities and how they could recognize God's presence in it.

CLOSING

Say: It's not always easy to do two things at once. But it *is* possible to have a great summer vacation *and* keep God first in our lives.

Close in prayer. ■

Be Prepared

■ **Theme:** New school year

■ **Scripture:** 1 Peter 3:15-16

■ **Overview:** Kids will take a test they're not ready for to help them see the importance of being ready to tell others about their faith.

■ **Preparation:** Put together a brief but extremely difficult test covering things the group has been studying recently. You'll need pencils, a song for the closing and a Bible.

EXPERIENCE

Without any warning, give kids the test you've prepared. Tell them you want to help them get used to tests since they'll soon be having them again in school. Ignore their complaining and make them take the test. Don't bother to correct the tests. Just ask: How did you feel not being prepared for this test? What could you have done to be more ready for it?

Read 1 Peter 3:15-16. Ask: How is being ready to tell someone about your faith like being ready for a test?

RESPONSE

Say: God doesn't expect us to be theologians, but he does want us to be ready to tell others what our faith means to us. And he may send someone our way who's curious about Christianity. As you start a new school year, think about what you'd do if someone asked you what you believe.

Form pairs and give partners each one minute to tell their partner what their faith means to them. Call time at the end of each minute.

After both partners have shared, ask: How hard was it to tell about your faith? Why? How can you be more ready to talk to someone who's interested in what you believe?

Be Prepared

CLOSING

Sing "Awesome God" or "I'm Yours" from *The Group Songbook* (Group Books) to help kids think about who God is and what he means to them. Offer to help kids who are interested in learning more about how to tell others what it means to be a Christian. ■

A Note of Thanks

■ **Theme:** Thanksgiving

■ **Scripture:** Luke 17:11-19

■ **Overview:** Group members will write thank-you notes to individuals who have made a positive difference in their lives.

■ **Preparation:** Gather a 2-foot piece of string, a sheet of stationery, a pen and an envelope for each group member. You'll also need a Bible.

EXPERIENCE

Distribute pieces of string and gather everyone in a circle on the floor. Say: Think about the nicest thing anyone has done for you recently—something you thought was especially kind or thoughtful. It might be something the person wasn't even aware that you appreciated. Use your string to make an outline on the floor that represents that act of kindness.

Allow about two minutes for kids to create their outlines. Then have kids take turns telling about their string outlines and the acts of kindness they represent.

RESPONSE

Read Luke 17:11-19 aloud. Ask: What's unusual about this story?

Discuss the importance of giving thanks. Then ask: How many of you thanked the person who did the kind act you told about a few moments ago?

Say: Like the nine lepers who failed to say thanks to Jesus, we often forget to take time to say thanks to the people who touch our lives with kindness.

Distribute the stationery and envelopes and have kids each write a brief note of thanks to the person whose kind act they appreciated. Call time after four or five minutes. Encourage kids to finish their notes and mail them within 24 hours.

A Note of Thanks

CLOSING

Have everyone stand in a circle and hold hands. Say: We don't want to be like the nine lepers who took off without saying thank you. Let's remember to express our thanks to God every day.

Lead kids in an alphabet prayer of thanks. Call the letters of the alphabet one at a time and have kids respond by naming things they're thankful for that begin with each letter. ■

Get Ready!

■ **Theme:** Advent

■ **Scripture:** Isaiah 40:3-5

■ **Overview:** Group members will experience what it's like to be inadequately prepared for something, then choose one thing they'll do to prepare for Jesus' coming.

■ **Preparation:** You'll need a Bible, a jar of peanut butter, a loaf of bread and four knives.

EXPERIENCE

Form two groups and have each group sit in a circle. Give one group two knives. Give the other group a loaf of bread, two knives and a jar of peanut butter.

Say to both groups: Make peanut butter sandwiches for everyone in your group. Go ahead and start.

One group will easily make the sandwiches. The other group will obviously have problems! They may complain about not having the essential ingredients or try to steal bread and peanut butter from the other group. Or the other group may even offer to share its supplies. Just watch to see what happens.

RESPONSE

Bring everyone together. If the first group failed to get the necessary ingredients, have the second group share their bread and peanut butter now. As kids eat their sandwiches ask: What was your first reaction when I explained what was going to happen? How did it feel to be in the group that wasn't properly prepared to carry out my instructions? What were the consequences of not being prepared? What were the benefits of being prepared?

Ask someone to read aloud Isaiah 40:3-5. Ask: What do we need to do to be prepared for the coming of the Lord into our lives? into our world? What keeps us from being prepared? What are the consequences of not being prepared?

Have kids each tell one thing they can do to prepare the way for Jesus' coming into their lives or into the world.

Get Ready!

CLOSING

Join hands and pray: Lord, help us pave the path for you. Help us to take time now to get ready. Here we are, Lord. We're ready to take that first step. Amen. ■

What's in a Name?

■ **Theme:** Christmas
■ **Scripture:** Isaiah 9:6
■ **Overview:** Group members will have a chance to learn about their names and the names of Jesus.
■ **Preparation:** Get a book at your local library that tells the meanings of names. You'll also need a recording of Handel's *Messiah* that includes the chorus "For Unto Us a Child Is Born," a CD or cassette player, pencils, one slip of paper for each student, a container for the paper slips, and a Bible.

EXPERIENCE

As kids come in have them each write their name on a slip of paper. Collect the papers in a container. Pull names out at random and look up their meanings. Share the meanings with the group.

RESPONSE

Ask: How did it feel to hear the meaning of your name? Does the meaning reflect your personality? If you could choose a new name for yourself, what would it be? Explain.

Read Isaiah 9:6. Explain that these are some of the names that God used to describe his son Jesus and announce his coming birth. Ask: How do these names reflect the personality of Jesus? If you were to announce the birth of Christ, what names would you use to describe the coming savior?

CLOSING

Tell the group that over 200 years ago a man named George Frederick Handel put this verse from Isaiah to music. Close the devotion by playing the recording of "For Unto Us a Child Is Born" from Handel's *Messiah*. Ask kids to be in an attitude of worship as they listen. ■

Bible Study Series

Give Your Teenagers a Solid Faith Foundation That Lasts a Lifetime!

Here are the *essentials* of the Christian life—core values teenagers *must* believe to make good decisions now...and build an *unshakable* lifelong faith. Developed by youth workers like you...field-tested with *real* youth groups in *real* churches...here's the meat your kids *must* have to grow spiritually—presented in a fun, involving way!

Each 4-session **Core Belief Bible Study Series** book lets you easily...

● Lead deep, compelling, *relevant* discussions your kids won't want to miss...

● Involve teenagers in exploring life-changing truths...

● Help kids create healthy relationships with each other—and you!

Plus you'll make an *eternal difference* in the lives of your kids as you give them a solid faith foundation that stands firm on God's Word.

Here are the Core Belief Bible Study Series titles already available...

Senior High Studies

Why **Authority** Matters	0-7644-0892-5
Why **Being a Christian** Matters	0-7644-0883-6
Why **Creation** Matters	0-7644-0880-1
Why **Forgiveness** Matters	0-7644-0887-9
Why **God** Matters	0-7644-0874-7
Why **God's Justice** Matters	0-7644-0886-0
Why **Jesus Christ** Matters	0-7644-0875-5
Why **Love** Matters	0-7644-0889-5
Why **Our Families** Matter	0-7644-0894-1
Why **Personal Character** Matters	0-7644-0885-2
Why **Prayer** Matters	0-7644-0893-3
Why **Relationships** Matter	0-7644-0896-8
Why **Serving Others** Matters	0-7644-0895-X
Why **Spiritual Growth** Matters	0-7644-0884-4
Why **Suffering** Matters	0-7644-0879-8
Why **the Bible** Matters	0-7644-0882-8
Why **the Church** Matters	0-7644-0890-9
Why **the Holy Spirit** Matters	0-7644-0876-3
Why **the Last Days** Matter	0-7644-0888-7
Why **the Spiritual Realm** Matters	0-7644-0881-X
Why **Worship** Matters	0-7644-0891-7

Junior High/Middle School Studies

The Truth About **Authority**	0-7644-0868-2
The Truth About **Being a Christian**	0-7644-0859-3
The Truth About **Creation**	0-7644-0856-9
The Truth About **Developing Character**	0-7644-0861-5
The Truth About **God**	0-7644-0850-X
The Truth About **God's Justice**	0-7644-0862-3
The Truth About **Jesus Christ**	0-7644-0851-8
The Truth About **Love**	0-7644-0865-8
The Truth About **Our Families**	0-7644-0870-4
The Truth About **Prayer**	0-7644-0869-0
The Truth About **Relationships**	0-7644-0872-0
The Truth About **Serving Others**	0-7644-0871-2
The Truth About **Sin and Forgiveness**	0-7644-0863-1
The Truth About **Spiritual Growth**	0-7644-0860-7
The Truth About **Suffering**	0-7644-0855-0
The Truth About **the Bible**	0-7644-0858-5
The Truth About **the Church**	0-7644-0899-2
The Truth About **the Holy Spirit**	0-7644-0852-6
The Truth About **the Last Days**	0-7644-0864-X
The Truth About **the Spiritual Realm**	0-7644-0857-7
The Truth About **Worship**	0-7644-0867-4

Order today from your local Christian bookstore, or write:
Group Publishing, P.O. Box 485, Loveland, CO 80539.

MORE INNOVATIVE RESOURCES FOR YOUR YOUTH MINISTRY

The Youth Worker's Encyclopedia of Bible-Teaching Ideas: Old Testament/ New Testament

Explore the most comprehensive idea-books available for youth workers! Discover more than 360 creative ideas in each encyclopedia—there's at least one idea for each and every book of the Bible. Find ideas for...retreats and overnighters, learning games, adventures, special projects, parties, prayers, music, devotions, skits, and much more!

Plus, you can use these ideas for groups of all sizes in any setting. Discover exciting new ways to teach each book of the Bible to your youth group.

Old Testament	ISBN 1-55945-184-X
New Testament	ISBN 1-55945-183-1

Clip-Art Cartoons for Churches

Here are over 180 funny, photocopiable illustrations to help you jazz up your calendars, newsletters, posters, fliers, transparencies, postcards, business cards, announcements—all your printed materials! These fun, fresh illustrations cover a variety of church and Christian themes, including church life, Sunday school, youth groups, school life, sermons, church events, volunteers, and more!

Each illustration is provided in the sizes you need most, so it's easy to use. Order your copy of **Clip-Art Cartoons for Churches** today...and add some spice to your next printed piece.

ISBN 1-55945-791-0

Bore No More! (For Every Pastor, Speaker, Teacher)

This book is a must for every pastor, youth leader, teacher, and speaker. These 70 audience-grabbing activities pull listeners into your lesson or sermon—and drive your message home!

Discover clever object lessons, creative skits, and readings. Music and celebration ideas. Affirmation activities. All the innovative techniques 85 percent of adult churchgoers say they wish their pastors would try! (recent Group Publishing poll)

Involve your congregation in the learning process! Order today! ISBN 1-55945-266-8

Order today from your local Christian bookstore, or write:
Group Publishing, Box 485, Loveland, CO 80539.